10. Happiness Experiments

from The Happiness Lab

by Paul Griffiths

Copyright © 2016 Paul Griffiths
This edition copyright © 2016 Ugly Duckling Publishing

The right of Paul Griffiths to be identified as the author of this work [and Matt Hewis to be identified as the illustrator of this work] has been asserted by him in accordance with the Copyright, Designs and Patents Act 1988.

All rights reserved. No part of this publication may be reproduced or transmitted in any form or by any means, electronic or mechanical, including photocopy, recording, or any information storage and retrieval system, without permission in writing from the publisher.

Published by Ugly Duckling Publishing
Claremont House
Lydney
Gloucestershire
GL15 5DX
Email: office@theuglyducklingcompany.com
www.thehappinesslab.org

ISBN 978-0-9935922-0-1

First edition 2016
Printed and bound in UK

Acknowledgements
Christian Brumwell (Initial Editing), Sharon Lanfear,
Miranda Lever (Editor), Paul Worthy (Designer)

Set in 14pt Adobe Garamond Pro

FOREWORD

Happiness is the holy grail of contemporary culture.

Experts tell us that our happiness level is made up of primarily three factors: 50% relates to our DNA and is considered to be fairly set; 10% is determined by our current situation and 40% is shaped by our life practices that can alter our happiness level so that it goes up or down.

The Happiness Lab was set up to explore what practices we should be building into our lives to raise our happiness level. Our intention is to look at what the wisdom of the ages, cultural trends, tribal insights and modern day experts have to say about happiness.

This book is not a one size fits all programme to make you a happier person, but rather sets out 101 ideas for you to experiment with to see what makes you happier.

101 Happiness Experiments

from The Happiness Lab

Hug.

Celebrate the achievements
of family members.

Take inspiration from one
of your heroes.

Use your words to inspire and encourage others.

Be intentional about listening to others.

Spend time with a soul friend.

Develop rituals for saying
"goodbye" and "hello".

Pamper yourself.

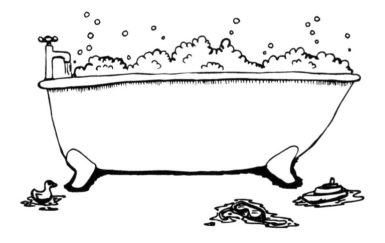

Admire the beauty around you.

Identify one reason for each letter of the alphabet for why you can be thankful today.

Choreograph your own gratitude dance, and when good things happen, take to life's dance floor.

Engage all your senses in the moments of today.

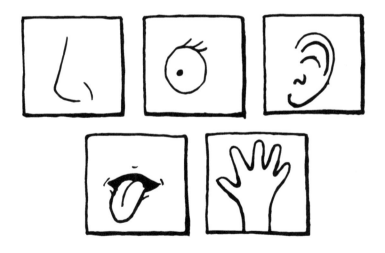

Detox from social media
for a little while.

Spend time with someone who will listen.

Go for a walk and savour the journey.

Give someone your place in the queue.

Enjoy the company and memories
of older members of your
community or family.

Use your camera to start capturing inspiring moments.

Going on holiday? Read about it before you go. Take moments to stop during your break. Savour it upon your return.

Plan a date night.

Spend 10 minutes today thinking about your most precious possession… Why is it precious; what is the story behind it?

Thank a mentor.

> Dear Grandad,
>   You have been such a huge influence in my life and I wanted to say thank you.

Keep a gratitude journal.

Daydream about what gives you hope.

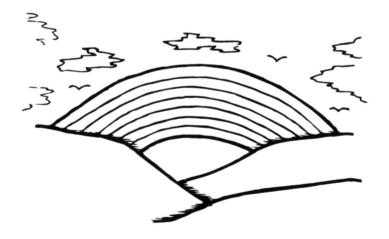

Talk to yourself about your good points.

Celebrate special days.

Anticipate the next good thing
that will be happening.

Reminisce with people
important to you.

Purchase and display a holiday souvenir, and think about your time away whenever you see it.

Write a poem about one of your favourite memories.

Go on a retreat.

Talk to someone who has been forgiven.

Say "thank you" more often.

Schedule holiday activities
into every month.

Stargaze.

Listen to your favourite piece of music.

Fundraise for a cause you believe in.

Give an unexpected gift to someone.

Meaningfully pass on to others
what you no longer need.

Go sit in a graveyard and consider
your own life and time.

Question your own thoughts and attitudes about a negative situation.

Go on an adventure with a friend.

Enrol in a new class and
learn a new skill.

Enjoy a sunrise or sunset.

Practise acts of kindness.

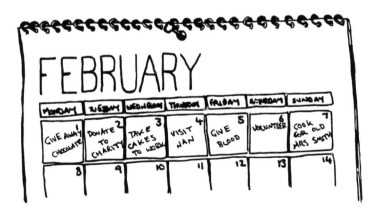

Create a memory box.

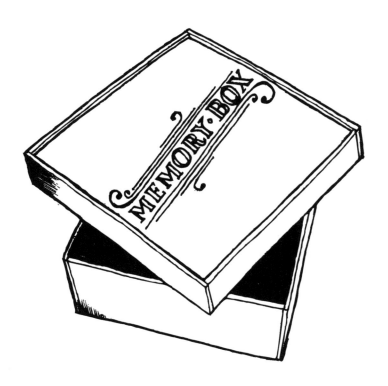

Meditate.

Celebrate your own successes.

Plan a simple day.

Be anonymously kind to a neighbour.

Check: Have you tagged your life's possessions with the right values?

Watch an inspiring film.

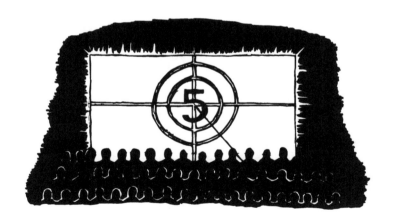

Actively store up happy memories
for when times are tough.

Support someone less fortunate than yourself.

Reflect on some of life's tougher times
and what you can learn from them.

Binge out on your favourite TV series.

Give yourself permission to be happy.

Cheer others on.

Find opportunities through the day to serve others.

Identify what stops you from
savouring a situation.

Appreciate the good people who make up your day.

Express appreciation to members of your family.

Think about who has
influenced you for good.

Appropriately and wisely try and deal with the difficult people in your life.

Choose your own gratitude song
and sing it out when life is good.

Laugh.

Practise kindness in the home.

Don't try to keep up with the Joneses.

Create an action plan to deal with
an issue that concerns you.

Not forgiving someone can make us sad, develop your forgiveness muscles by thinking about someone who forgave you.

Invest your wisdom in the
young generation.

Visit your local art gallery and admire the paintings.

Say grace more often, like before going to watch a great film or play.

Create and practise family traditions.

Learn to say no when you need to.

Appreciate the eternal worth
of what you do now.

Mark special moments.

Plan a quiet day.

Not forgiving someone can make us sad,
imagine offering forgiveness to someone.

Develop a good bedtime routine
that enables you to sleep.

Pray.

Take mental photographs.

Take 10 minutes to look through a
photo album and reminisce.

Tell everyone your good news.

Smile more.

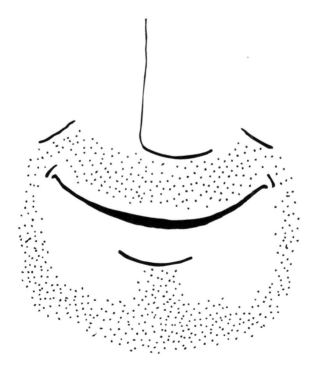

Develop a worldview that makes
sense of the world you live in.

Engage in appropriate physical exercise.

Enthusiastically celebrate the achievements of others.

Spend time with family and friends during tough times.

Take time to compliment someone.

Not forgiving someone can make us sad – not everyone should be forgiven – offer forgiveness to someone who has hurt you.

Read an inspiring novel or watch a gripping film that tells the story of one person's journey of offering forgiveness.

Find space during a tough day.

Find a place to belong spiritually.

Offer support to someone going through a tough time.

Think through what brings
meaning to your life.

Eat slower with others.

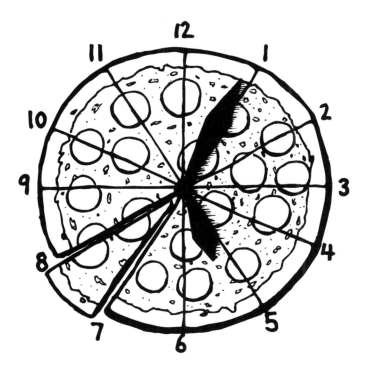

Focus on what you do have rather than what you don't have.

LIFE INVENTORY

1.

2.

3.

4.

5.

Find your own sacred space and
visit as often as possible.

Bake someone a cake.

Plan the perfect day.

The Happiness Lab

The Happiness Lab is a six week programme, giving you the opportunity to explore what psychologies, doctors and faith leaders have to say about happiness.

For more information visit www.thehappinesslab.org

The 8 Secrets of Happiness

Paul Griffiths & Martin Robinson

The twenty-first century is a century of limitless possibilities. We are surrounded by innumerable products promising to make us healthier, more intelligent, more popular and more successful. But somehow it's not quite enough – there's more to happiness than having a great job, designer clothes, a busy social life or a fat bank balance.

This book will guide you through the eight secrets that psychologists have discovered to be the foundations of happiness, revealing a hidden dimension they all share. In an age of unprecedented wealth, coupled with unprecedented unhappiness and even depression, this book is a wake up call. It's time to rediscover happiness – and here's how.

This book is available as:
an iBook from iTunes
a Kindle edition from Amazon

Published by Lion Hudson

Milton Keynes UK
Ingram Content Group UK Ltd.
UKHW020005131023
430453UK00004B/42